From the Earth to the Stars

By George Ivanoff

Pearson Australia
(a division of Pearson Australia Group Pty Ltd)
707 Collins Street, Melbourne, Victoria 3008
PO Box 23360, Melbourne, Victoria 8012
www.pearson.com.au

First published 2014 by Pearson Australia
2020 2019 2018 2017
10 9 8 7 6 5 4 3 2 1

Publisher: Kieren Noonan
Project Managers: Tamara Pirois and Rachel Davis
Lead Editors: Kerry Nagle and Beth Zeme
Editor: Carolyn Glascodine
Cover and Series Designers: Jenny Grigg and Anne Donald
Designers: Nina Heryanto and Norma van Rees
Copyright & Pictures Editor: Julia Weaver
Mac Operator: Rob Curulli
Illustrator: Fiona Lee
Printed in Australia by the SOS Print + Media Group

ISBN 978 1 4860 0772 1
Pearson Australia Group Pty Ltd ABN 40 004 245 943

Acknowledgements
We would like to thank the following for permission to reproduce copyright material.
The following abbreviations are used in this list: t = top, b = bottom, l = left, r = right, c = centre.

Alamy Ltd: Radius Images, p. 11bl; Excitations, p. 13. Dreamstime: p. 10. Fairfax Photo Sales: Fairfax Media Publications Pty Limited, p. 20tr. Getty Images: SPL Creative, pp. 5, 11tr. Mars One: Bryan Versteeg, p. 29. NASA Images : Courtesy of nasaimages.org, pp. Front cover, 8, 15r, 24, 26, 27, 28. Pearson Asset Library: pp. 25, 30. Shutterstock: pp. 1, 3, 4, 6t, 6b, 11br, 12, 14l, 14r, 15l, 16, 18, 19, 20bl, 21, 23, back cover.

Disclaimer
Some of the images used in *From the Earth to the Stars* might have associations with deceased Indigenous Australians. Please be aware that these images might cause sadness or distress in Aboriginal or Torres Strait Islander communities.

Contents

Up and beyond!

The Earth is the third of eight planets that **orbit** a star. That star is known as the Sun.

The Sun is the centre of our solar system, which is made up of everything that orbits it. As well as the eight planets, there are dwarf planets, **asteroids**, comets and other smaller bodies circling the Sun. Scientists believe that our solar system is more than four billion years old.

Our solar system, in turn, forms part of the Milky Way **galaxy**, which contains 200 billion stars. And this galaxy is just one of billions in the **Universe**.

The Earth really is just one tiny cosmic speck. But it's unique, because it is able to support life.

To understand the Earth and the changes it goes through, it is necessary to understand its place in the solar system and in the Universe as a whole.

LET'S FIND OUT

- What is the Earth's place within the solar system?
- What is the importance of the Sun to the Earth and the solar system?
- How has our understanding of the solar system and the Universe changed over time?
- Why is discovery and exploration of space so important?
- Who has contributed to our understanding of the solar system and the Universe?

The Milky Way galaxy and our solar system

The fire in the sky

Sol is the Latin name for the Sun, and is the basis of the word *solar*.

The Sun emits light and warmth, and without it, life could not exist on Earth. So it's not surprising that early humans worshipped the Sun as a god and made up myths about it.

Ancient myths

To the ancient Greeks, Helios was the god who embodied the Sun. He was said to drive the chariot of the Sun across the sky each day.

In ancient Egyptian mythology, the Sun represented light, warmth and growth, so the Sun god Ra was very important to ancient Egyptians. They believed that he travelled in a boat through the sky during the day and through the Underworld at night. This explained the rising and setting of the Sun.

The Aztec people of Mexico had five Sun gods ruling in turn. They believed that the Sun gods demanded human sacrifices and that the Sun would not rise without those sacrifices.

The Aztec calendar stone is called the 'Stone of the Sun'.

The statue of Ra at an Egyptian temple

The Earth and the Sun

The Earth travels around the Sun in an **elliptical** orbit. As it orbits the Sun, the Earth rotates. The part of the Earth that faces the Sun is in daytime, while the other half is in night time.

At the same time, the Earth spins on its **axis**, which is tilted, and this is what causes the seasons. Different parts of the Earth face the Sun at different times of the year. When the Southern Hemisphere is tilted more towards the Sun, the Sun rises higher in the sky and is above the horizon longer. This is when we have summer and longer days. When the Southern Hemisphere is tilted away from the Sun, we have winter and shorter days.

While the Southern Hemisphere is tilted towards the Sun, the Northern Hemisphere is tilted away from it. This means the seasons are opposite in the Northern and Southern hemispheres.

We have seasons because the Earth spins on its axis as it orbits the Sun.

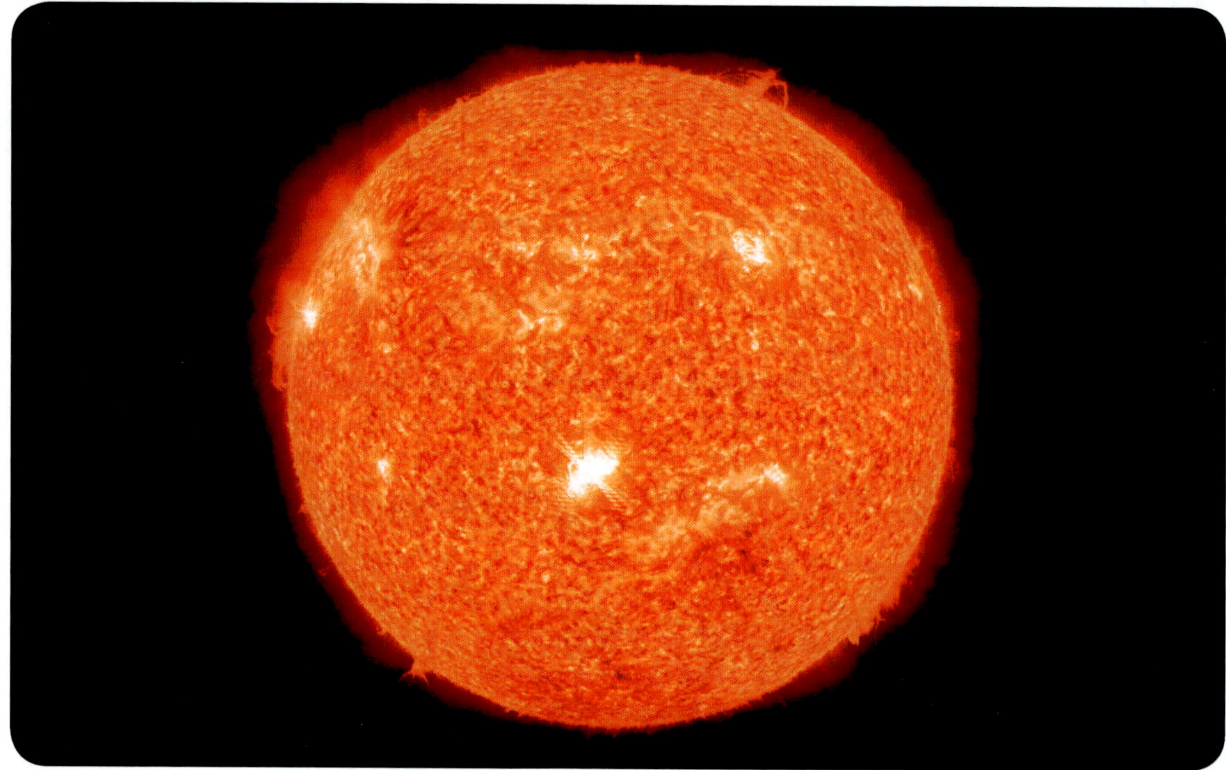

The Sun

Sun facts

The Sun is 150 million kilometres from the Earth.

The Sun has a diameter of 1.4 million kilometres, which is about 100 times the diameter of the Earth.

The Sun is mostly made up of **hydrogen**. The rest is mostly the light gas helium, with about 0.1 per cent made up of carbon, nitrogen, oxygen, neon, magnesium, silicon and iron.

Creating energy

The Sun gives off energy in the form of light, heat, ultraviolet light and radio waves. This energy is created through a process called 'thermonuclear fusion'.

In the superheated core of the Sun (about 16 million degrees Celsius), helium is created from hydrogen. This process releases energy. The energy travels to the surface of the Sun and radiates out, providing light and heat to the planets around it.

The surface of the Sun is a lot cooler. It's only about 5500 degrees Celsius. That's still pretty hot – much too hot and bright to look at. Looking directly at the Sun can damage our eyes, so scientists study the Sun through special telescopes.

Solar eclipse

A solar **eclipse** is a fascinating and rare event. It happens when the Moon passes between the Sun and Earth. The Moon fully or partially blocks our view of the Sun.

When you look at a solar eclipse (using safety goggles), the Sun and the Moon look about the same size. In fact, the Sun is approximately 400 times larger than the Moon. But because the Sun is almost 400 times further away, the Sun and Moon look about the same size from Earth.

Did you know?

The Sun is the largest object in the solar system. A million Earths could fit inside it. The Sun makes up 98 per cent of all matter in the solar system. This means that everything else, including all the planets, makes up only 2 per cent.

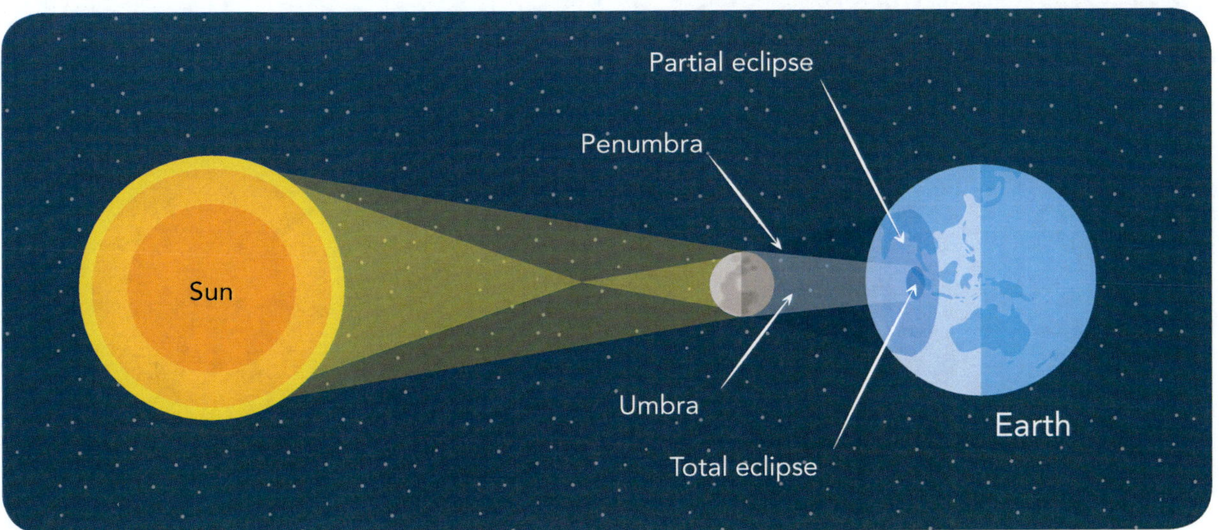

The position of the Earth, the Moon and the Sun during a solar eclipse

In the night sky

The Sun is so bright that during the day, you can't see other sources of light in the sky. But in the night sky, without the light of the Sun, you can see specks of light. These are stars – just like our Sun, but much further away.

Stars

The nearest star to Earth, other than the Sun, is Proxima Centauri. It's a little over four **light-years** away. It's small and not as bright as our Sun. In fact, it's too faint to see with the naked eye. It was discovered in 1915 by astronomer Robert Innes, using a telescope at the Union Observatory in South Africa.

The second and third closest stars are Alpha Centauri A and B. They are **binary** stars, which means they are part of the same system. They are close enough to each other to appear as a single star (the third brightest) in the night sky.

The night sky is full of stars.

The brightest star in the night sky is Sirius, also known as the Dog Star. At 8.6 light-years away, it is the sixth closest star to our solar system. It is almost twice as bright as the next brightest star, Canopus.

Through the ages, people from around the world have grouped the stars into patterns called 'constellations'. Today, in modern **astronomy**, there are 88 constellations.

Scorpius (also known as Scorpio) is one of the brightest constellations in the sky. It is made up of 18 main stars, but many more stars are officially part of the constellation. Its brightest star is Antares.

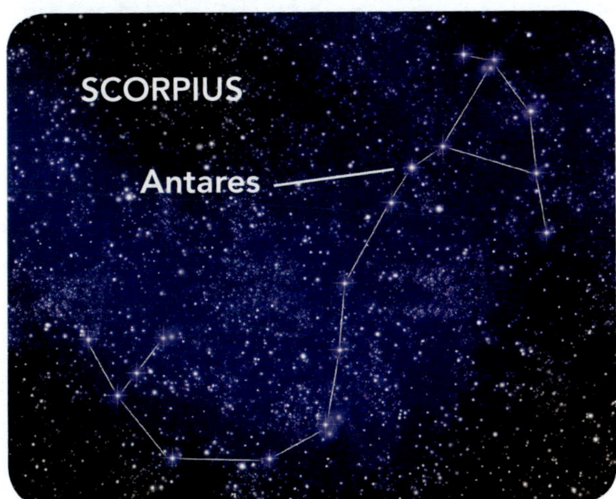

The constellation Scorpius

The constellation Southern Cross

Another constellation that you might already be familiar with is the Southern Cross, also known as Crux. It's the easiest constellation to see in the Southern Hemisphere. The five stars on the Australian and New Zealand flags represent the Southern Cross.

The Australian flag

Planets

There are more than just stars in the night sky. We can also see planets and the Moon. Although these bodies do not produce their own light, they reflect the light of the Sun.

Most of the planets in our solar system can be seen in the sky. Venus is the brightest and is sometimes called the 'morning star' or 'evening star'. Mercury, Mars, Jupiter and Saturn can also be seen without a telescope. Uranus can sometimes be seen, but it's hard to spot. Neptune is too faint to be seen with the naked eye.

The Moon

By far the most noticeable object in the night sky is the Moon. It reflects the light of the Sun, which is why we can see it at night and sometimes during the day. The amount of reflected light is what causes the phases of the Moon – from full Moon to crescent Moon.

Did you know?

The Moon's **gravity** affects the Earth. The Earth's gravity is greater, so the Moon is kept in orbit around the Earth. But the Moon's gravitational pull influences the oceans' tides.

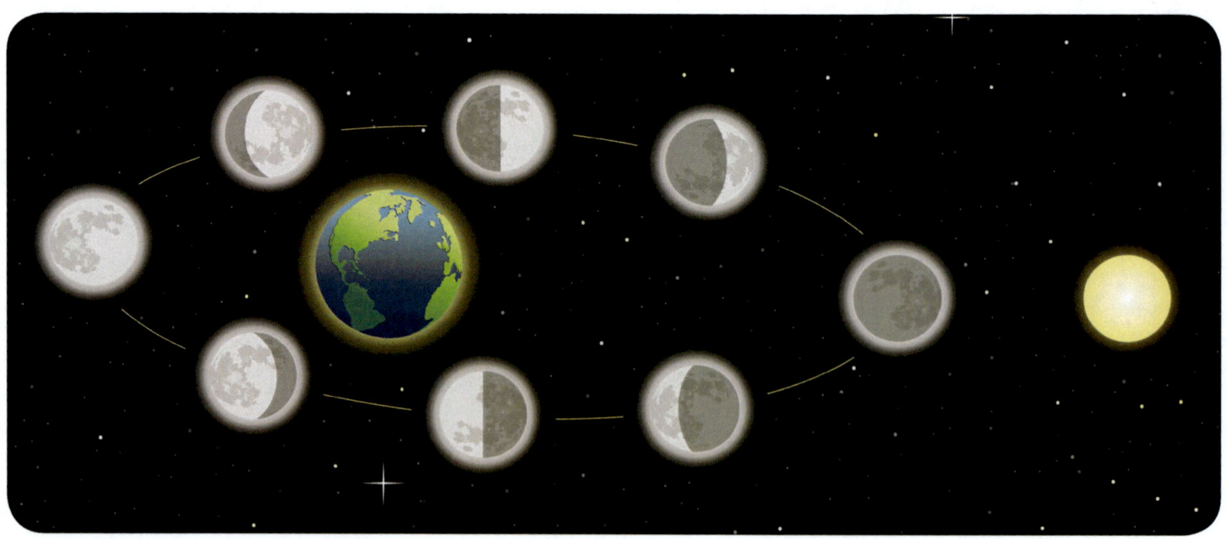

The phases of the Moon

Also in the night sky

You can sometimes spot shooting stars in the night sky. They look like stars moving quickly across the sky. In reality they are **meteors**, burning up in the Earth's atmosphere.

A comet is a frozen mass of gases, rock and dust (a bit like a cosmic snowball), orbiting the Sun. Sometimes, a comet's orbit will take it close enough to Earth to be seen in the night sky. A comet's dust reflects the Sun's light, so a comet often appears to have a halo and a glowing tail. Comets are rare, and there are often many years between sightings.

Perhaps the most famous is Halley's Comet, last seen in 1986. But there have been other comets, including Comet Hyakutake (1996), Comet Hale–Bopp (1997) and Comet McNaught (2007).

The Comet McNaught

Through the lens

When most people think of a telescope, they think of an instrument that makes faraway objects appear closer. That is an optical telescope. There are many other types of telescopes – radio telescopes, X-ray telescopes, ultraviolet telescopes and infrared telescopes. These telescopes also help the user observe objects that are far away.

The first optical telescope was made in the Netherlands in 1608. Italian scientist Galileo Galilei made his own in 1609, improving on the Dutch design. During the 20th century, other types of telescopes were invented.

Galileo Galilei

A reflector telescope can be used to view the night sky.

Astronomers use telescopes to observe objects in our solar system and beyond. Telescopes have helped astronomers discover planets and their moons, comets and asteroids. They have helped astronomers discover details about these objects, including their size and distance from Earth.

Without the telescope, we would know a lot less about our solar system.

Telescopes come in all shapes and sizes – from a small telescope on a tripod to a gigantic telescope housed in its own building called an 'observatory'. There are even telescopes out in space.

The new VISTA telescope in Chile is the largest telescope in the world.

Space agencies have been putting telescopes into space since the 1970s. The best-known space telescope is the Hubble Space Telescope. It is an optical telescope, which was carried into the Earth's orbit by a space

The Hubble Space Telescope

shuttle in 1990. Despite some early problems, this telescope has been widely used. For example, it showed the collision of a comet with Jupiter in 1994.

Astronauts have to keep the Hubble Space Telescope in working order. There have been five space missions to repair and upgrade the telescope.

Did you know?
The rings of Saturn were first seen by Galileo through a telescope in 1610. Before that, no one knew that they even existed.

The planets

Using telescopes, astronomers have discovered many things about the planets in our solar system.

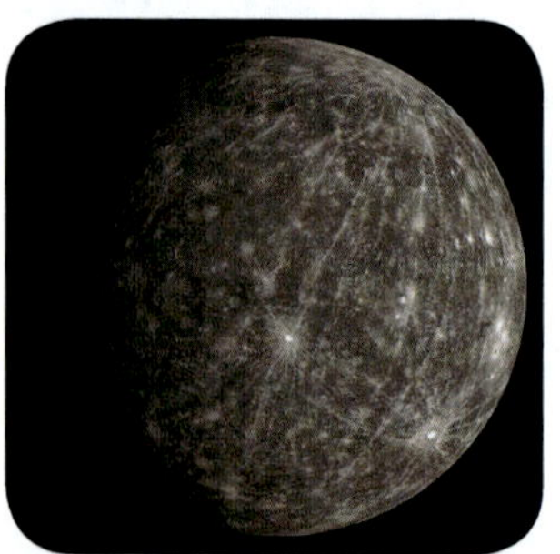

Mercury

Named after the ancient Roman messenger god, because he was fast.

Circumference: 15 329.1 km (smallest planet)
Orbit length: 87.97 Earth days (fastest orbit)
Temperature: 427°C to –179°C
Moons: 0

Venus

Named after the ancient Roman goddess of beauty, because it was the brightest planet in the night sky.

Circumference: 38 024.6 km (almost the same as Earth)
Orbit length: 224.70 Earth days
Temperature: over 462°C
Moons: 0

Earth

Earth is an English/German word, which simply means the ground. It is the only planet not named after a god.

Circumference: 40 030.2 km
Orbit length: 1 year
Temperature: 58°C to –88°C
Moons: 1

Mars

Named after the Roman god of war, because of its blood red colour.

Circumference: 21 296.9 km (about half the size of Earth)
Orbit length: 686.98 Earth days
Temperature: –87°C to –5°C
Moons: 2

Jupiter

Named after the main Roman god, because it is the largest planet.

Circumference: 439 263.8 km (largest planet: more than 1000 Earths would fit into Jupiter)
Orbit length: 4 332.82 Earth days
Temperature: about –148°C
Moons: over 50

Saturn

Named after the Roman god of agriculture.

Circumference: 365 882.4 km
Orbit length: 10 755.70 Earth days
Temperature: about –178 °C
Moons: over 50

Uranus

Named after the Greek god of the sky.

Circumference: 159 354.1 km
Orbit length: 30 687.15 Earth days
Temperature: about –216 °C
Moons: 27

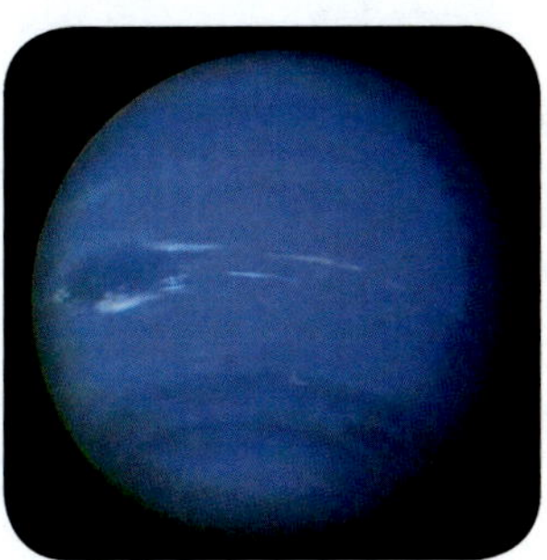

Neptune

Named after the Roman god of the sea.

Circumference: 154 704.6 km
Orbit length: 60 190.03 Earth days
Temperature: about –214 °C
Moons: 13

Astronomical discoveries

Astronomy is the study of objects in space (other than the Earth), such as planets, stars and asteroids.

In early times, astronomy simply involved looking up at the night sky, observing and predicting the movements of the visible objects. Astronomers created maps showing the positions of stars and planets.

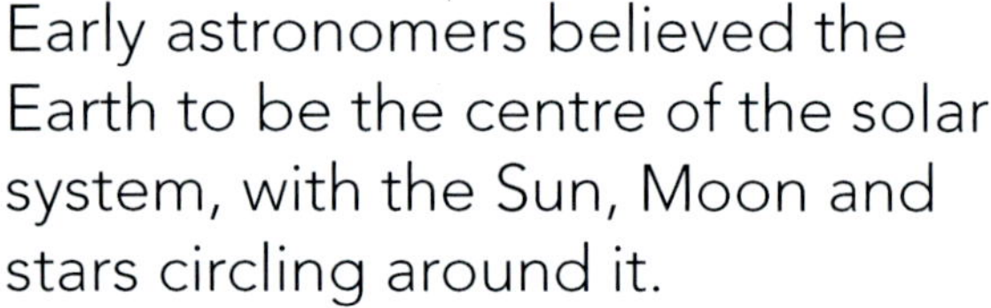

Early astronomers believed the Earth to be the centre of the solar system, with the Sun, Moon and stars circling around it.

In the 3rd century Before Common Era (BCE), ancient Greek astronomer Aristarchus of Samos was the first to suggest that the Earth went around the Sun.

In the 2nd century BCE, Hipparchus of Nicaea made many advances in astronomy. He calculated the size and distance of the Moon from Earth and invented the astrolabe, an instrument for locating and predicting the positions of stars and planets.

Despite the work of Aristarchus and other astronomers, most people still believed that everything revolved around the Earth.

It was the Polish astronomer Nicolaus Copernicus who challenged this in a book called *On the Revolutions of the Celestial Spheres* in 1543. He came up with a model, placing the Sun at the centre of the solar system. His work was continued by other astronomers, including Galileo.

The invention of the telescope greatly influenced astronomical discoveries. As new and better telescopes were developed, more discoveries were made.

Uranus and Neptune

Although the planet Uranus can be seen by the naked eye, it's very dim. Because of this and its slow orbit, early astronomers mistook it for a star. British astronomer William Herschel originally mistook it for a comet in 1781. But after further observation, using a new telescope that he had designed, Herschel realised that it was a planet.

Copernicus

Herschel

The discovery of Uranus led to the discovery of another planet, Neptune. In 1846, German astronomer Johann Gottfried Galle finally located Neptune with a telescope.

Uranus

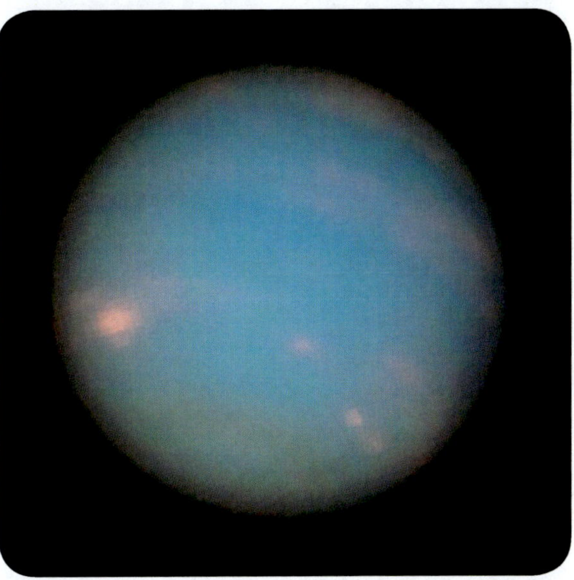

Neptune

Halley's Comet

In 1705, Edmund Halley discovered that the comets sighted in 1533, 1607 and 1682 were the same comet. He predicted it would return in 1758. It did, and it has been called 'Halley's Comet' ever since. The comet orbits the Sun, and every 75–76 years it is close enough to Earth to be seen. It was last seen in 1986. The next time humans will be able to see it is 2061.

Edmund Halley

Halley's Comet viewed from the Gawler Ranges in Adelaide in 1986

Missing planet

Our solar system used to have nine planets. But what ever happened to planet Pluto?

In the 1840s astronomers were studying the orbits of Uranus and Neptune. They predicted the existence of a ninth planet. In 1894 they began to look for this ninth planet, which they called 'Planet X'. In 1930 they found a small planet, which they called 'Pluto'. Some astronomers at the time felt it was too small to be called a planet.

In 2003, at the Palomar Observatory in California, USA, a new object about the same size as Pluto, was discovered in the outer part of our solar system. This led to a lot of discussion about what a planet was.

A new **classification** was finally created in 2006 – dwarf planet. The new object, named Eris, and Pluto were both classified as dwarf planets. The asteroid Ceres was also reclassified as a dwarf planet.

Since 2006, other bodies have been classified as dwarf planets, or are being considered for classification. Astronomers believe that there are many more dwarf planets waiting to be discovered.

Did you know?
Eris was nicknamed Xena while its name was being decided. Xena was the main character in *Xena: Warrior Princess*, a television series that was popular in the 1990s.

The dwarf planet Eris

Heading into space

Here is a time line of space exploration.

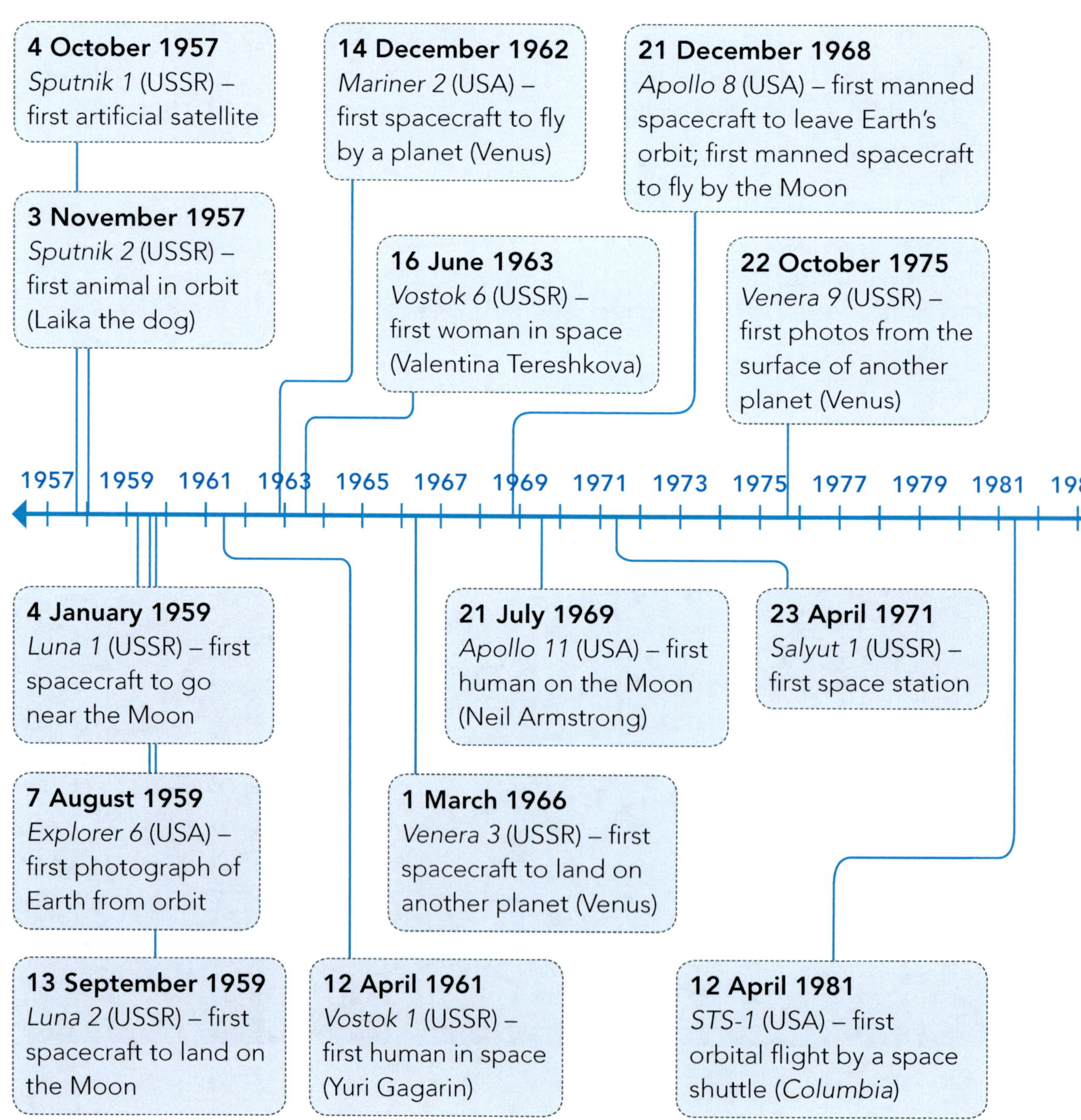

As well as observing objects in space through telescopes, humans have explored our solar system. Spacecraft have flown past the planets and photographed them. **Probes** have landed on Mars, Venus and Mercury. And people have also travelled into space, orbited the Earth, lived on space stations and visited the Moon.

It all started with *Sputnik 1*, the first artificial **satellite** to be launched into Earth's orbit in 1957.

1987 1989 1991 1993 1995 1997 1999 2001 2003 2005 2007 2009 2011 2013

19 February 1986
Mir (USSR) – first long-term research space station; first space station assembled in orbit

20 November 1998
ISS – construction of International Space Station begins

8 August 2012
Curiosity (USA) – nuclear-powered rover lands on Mars to look for signs of life

7 February 1984
STS-41-B (USA) – first **untethered** spacewalk (from the space shuttle *Columbia*)

6 March 2009
Kepler Mission (USA) – first space observatory designed to search for Earth-like planets outside our solar system

Many amazing discoveries have been made by sending spacecraft and people into space.

Voyager mission

In 1977, the US National Aeronautics and Space Administration, known as NASA, launched the two *Voyager* spacecraft on a long-term mission to explore the solar system and beyond. These two craft have made many discoveries and are still sending data back to Earth.

In 1979 *Voyager 1* discovered that the planet Jupiter has rings. There is a flat main ring, an inner cloud-like ring called the 'halo', and transparent outer rings, called the 'gossamer rings'. It also discovered volcanic activity on the Jovian moon, Io. In 1986 *Voyager 2* flew past Uranus and discovered an additional ten moons.

Space Shuttle Program

NASA's Space Shuttle Program produced a fleet of manned, reusable spacecraft. The test vehicle, *Enterprise* (named after the spaceship in the television series *Star Trek*), never made it into space.

The shuttles that did fly into space were *Columbia*, *Challenger*, *Discovery*, *Atlantis* and *Endeavour*.

Voyager 1 spacecraft

They carried out 135 missions between 1981 and 2011.

On 28 January 1986 the *Challenger* space shuttle exploded 73 seconds after take-off, killing all seven people on board. The disaster was caused by the failure of a seal in a rocket booster. On 1 February 2003, the *Columbia* space shuttle **disintegrated** during re-entry. This was caused when a piece of **insulation** fell off an external tank.

Despite these disasters, the Space Shuttle Program recovered and continued to launch missions until its closure in 2011. Shuttle missions put satellites into orbit, launched other spacecraft, helped construct the International Space Station, carried the Hubble Space Telescope into orbit and took scientists into space for research and experiments. The Space Shuttle Program included many firsts, such as America's first woman in space and the first untethered space walk.

Launch of space shuttle *Atlantis*

Did you know?
The first **civilian** astronaut, Sharon Christa McAuliffe, was a schoolteacher. She died in the *Challenger* space shuttle disaster in 1986.

To the future

We have discovered so much about our solar system over the years. Yet, there is still much to learn.

JAXA (Japan Aerospace Exploration Agency) has set its sights on the Moon. The unmanned *Selene* spacecraft was sent to the Moon in 2007. JAXA is now planning a manned mission by 2020, leading to a possible Moon base in the future.

NASA is continuing its exploration of Mars. The *Curiosity* Mars rover landed on the planet in August 2012 and is still sending data back to Earth. Another rover is planned for launch in 2020 and NASA is hoping to launch a manned mission in the 2030s.

NASA is planning a 2018 launch for the James Webb Space Telescope. This powerful infrared telescope will be used to study other galaxies. Older missions are also still in progress – returning new information to Earth. Launched in January 2006, the *New Horizons* spacecraft will reach the dwarf planet Pluto in 2015.

Engineers working on rovers to send to Mars

The International Space Station

Juno, launched in August 2011, will reach Jupiter in 2016. Launched in 2013, the Interface Region Imaging Spectrograph (IRIS) is a spacecraft that has been sent to observe the Sun.

International cooperation

The first multinational manned mission into space took place in 1975 – the US *Apollo* spacecraft docked with the Soviet *Soyuz* spacecraft.

The two spacecraft commanders exchanged the first international handshake in space, and the crews conducted joint scientific experiments.

Since then, there have been numerous multinational projects. The biggest multinational project was the International Space Station. The station was started in 1998 and completed in 2011. It is designed as a research laboratory, and will continue to operate for many years.

In the future, there may be more international cooperation, with exploration benefitting all people on Earth, not just one country.

Non-government space flight

Space flight and exploration has mostly been controlled by various governments through their space agencies. But there have been some private ventures funded by businesses.

In 2004, *SpaceShipOne* became the world's first privately built, manned spacecraft to fly into space. It was built by Mojave Aerospace Ventures in California, USA. *SpaceShipOne* was launched in mid-air from the *White Knight* jet-powered aircraft carrier.

Space tourists

Virgin Galactic is preparing to take tourists into space. The company has not yet announced when flights will begin, but they are already selling tickets. Over 500 tickets have already been sold. Scientist Stephen Hawking, singer Katy Perry and actors Brad Pitt and Angelina Jolie have already bought tickets. If you have a spare $200 000, you could buy a ticket.

Like *SpaceShipOne*, Virgin Galactic will also launch their spacecraft, named *SpaceShipTwo*, from an aircraft carrier.

SpaceShipOne

An artist's impresssion of a colony on Mars

Virgin Galactic also announced plans for *LauncherOne*, which will be able to send small satellites (100 kg and under) into the Earth's orbit. The aim is to be able to put satellites into space at a lower cost, allowing more groups such as universities and research programs to have access to space. It is estimated they will begin doing this in 2016.

Mars

There is also an ambitious private project that plans to send people to Mars by 2023. Mars One, a not-for-profit organisation, is also planning to establish a colony or settlement on Mars. Mars One merchandise is already on sale and a reality television series is planned to help raise money.

Did you know?
In 2001 millionaire businessman Dennis Tito paid $20 million to visit the International Space Station. Now he is planning his own Mars mission.

Connections

For hundreds of years, humans have been learning about the planet they live on, and the Universe.

We've learnt a great deal about Earth and its place within the solar system. Yet, there is still so much to discover and learn. There are many exploration projects being planned.

Maybe one day you will help to make further discoveries. Perhaps you will be an astronaut, piloting a spacecraft and exploring the solar system? Or an engineer, designing a new space probe that will journey to another star? Or an astronomer, looking through a telescope and observing the Universe?

One way to begin is by studying science and mathematics at high school. This is the basis you will need for a science or engineering degree at university.

And don't forget to keep watching the stars!

The night sky from Concana Observatory in Chile

Glossary

asteroids small bodies or rocks orbiting the Sun

astronomy the study of stars and planets

axis an invisible line around which something turns

binary double; in two parts

civilian a person not in the military, police or firefighting forces

classification organisation into groups based on shared characteristics

disintegrated broken into fragments

eclipse the obscuring of an astronomical object, such as the Sun or the Moon

elliptical oval-shaped

galaxy a system of millions of stars, held together by gravitational attraction

gravity the force of attraction between two objects

hydrogen a gas, with no smell or colour, which is highly flammable (likely to catch fire)

insulation material that protects against heat and/or cold

light-years the distance an object moving at the speed of light would travel in a year (around 10 trillion kilometres)

meteors small masses of rock from space that enter the Earth's atmosphere

orbit when an object in space moves around another on a regular path

probes unmanned craft designed for exploration

satellite a body or device that orbits a planet

shuttle a vehicle that goes back and forth

Universe all matter in space

untethered without a tether (rope or chain)

Index